PLAYING KEYBOARDS
CHILDREN'S SONGBOOK
BY ROGER EVANS
Easy music for all keyboards

Introduction	2
Playing Hints	2
Baa Baa, Black Sheep	4
Boys And Girls Come Out To Play	5
Goosey, Goosey Gander	6
The Grand Old Duke Of York	7
Here We Go Round The Mulberry Bush	8
Hey Diddle Diddle	9
Hickory Dickory Dock	10
Humpty Dumpty	11
Jack And Jill	12
Little Bo Peep	13
Little Jack Horner	14
Little Miss Muffet	14
London Bridge Is Falling Down	15
Mary, Mary, Quite Contrary	16
Michael Finnigin	17
Old MacDonald Had A Farm	18
One Man Went To Mow	19
Oranges And Lemons	20
Pat-A-Cake	21
Polly Put The Kettle On	22
Pop! Goes The Weasel	23
Rock-A-Bye Baby	24
She'll Be Coming Round The Mountain	25
Sing A Song Of Sixpence	26
Ten Green Bottles	27
There's A Hole In My Bucket	28
This Old Man	29
Three Blind Mice	30
Twinkle, Twinkle, Little Star	31

All music chosen and specially arranged by Roger Evans.

First Published 1986
© International Music Publications

Exclusive Distributors
International Music Publications
Southend Road, Woodford Green,
Essex IG8 8HN, England.

Photocopying of this copyright material is illegal.

215-2-375

Introduction

This entertaining collection of popular children's songs has been specially chosen to be fun to play and sing.

All the music has been arranged to be especially easy, and the songs are all in good singing keys.

You can play all of the songs in this book with 'One Finger Chords', 'Casio Chords' or 'Single Finger Chords' — or you can use 'Fingered Chords'. In fact, only five easy chords are needed to play all of the music in this book!

Most of the music is also suitable for other instruments like the guitar, recorder and violin, so your family or friends can play along with you if you wish.

Just follow these helpful hints, and you can quickly start enjoying the music:

Playing Hints

The music in this book follows the same easy style used in all *Playing Keyboards* books:

Suggested Voices and Rhythms are given at the beginning of every tune, like this:

> Guitar/Piano
> Ballad/Pops or Rock (Medium)

You can choose whichever settings suit your keyboard. Here, you could choose either the Guitar or Piano voice, and set a Ballad, Pops or Rock rhythm.

If your keyboard does not have any of the suggested voices or rhythms, choose voices and rhythms which suit the music you are playing.

The suggested Tempo (speed) of the music is given in brackets: (Medium). Adjust the Tempo control on your keyboard to this suggested setting before you begin each tune. (If you like, set the Tempo slower than suggested until you are comfortable playing a new tune).

Fingering — Finger numbers are shown in front of notes where the fingering is not obvious, and where the fingers need to move to different keys:

> 1 = thumb   2 = index finger   3 = middle finger   4 = ring finger   5 = little finger

Special Effects which you can add to the music are shown in brackets over some tunes:

(Arpeggio) — means you can add an automatic 'Arpeggio' to the backing of a tune, if your keyboard has this effect.

Chords — Chord 'symbols' are shown over the music wherever a chord change is needed.

Playing For Singing: You can play the melody, chords and rhythm together in the usual way to accompany singing. However, it is often very effective (and easier) to play just the chords and rhythm on their own as the backing for some songs. This allows you to concentrate on the singing without worrying about playing the melody. When you do this, you can rest your right hand, or use it to play solos or fill-in notes between the verses of the song.

Try to hear the tune in your head before you begin playing, and adjust the rhythm to the right 'speed' by watching the Tempo Lamp on your keyboard as it flashes in time with the beat.

Play the first note of the song to give the 'starting note' for singing. Even better, play the last part or first part of the tune to lead in the singing. This works very well for most tunes.

If any songs are too high or too low for a singer, you could use the transposer (if your keyboard has one) to adjust the pitch:

If the music is too high for the singer, try setting the transposer to B♭ (-2) or G (-5).
If the music is too low, set the transposer to E♭ (+3) or F (+5).

Synchro Start: Press the 'Synchro Start' or 'Synchro' button on your keyboard before you begin, so the rhythm starts automatically when you play the first chord.

You may prefer some of the songs without an automatic rhythm. Play them both ways, with and without rhythm, and make your own choice. (Do not press 'Synchro Start' if you want to play chords without an automatic rhythm.)

You can find more playing hints, easy-to-follow instruction and more good tunes to play in the *Playing Keyboards* book and cassette, obtainable from your music dealer.

Have fun singing and playing all the songs in this book.

Roger Evans

Baa Baa, Black Sheep

Violin/Strings
Ballad/Pops or Rock (Medium)

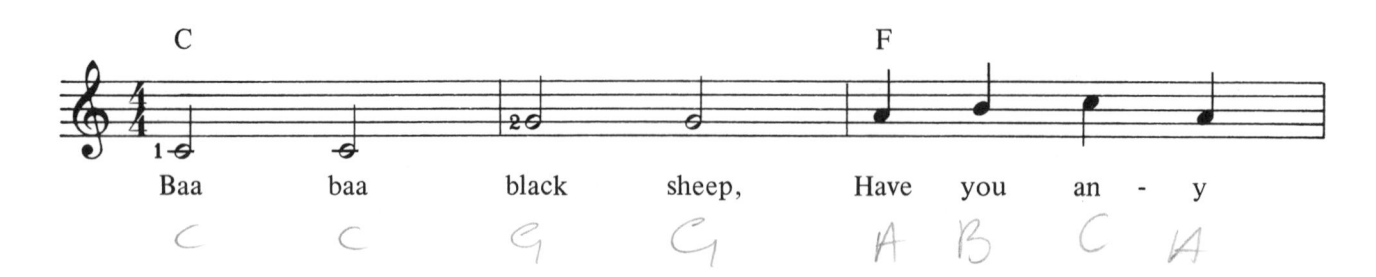

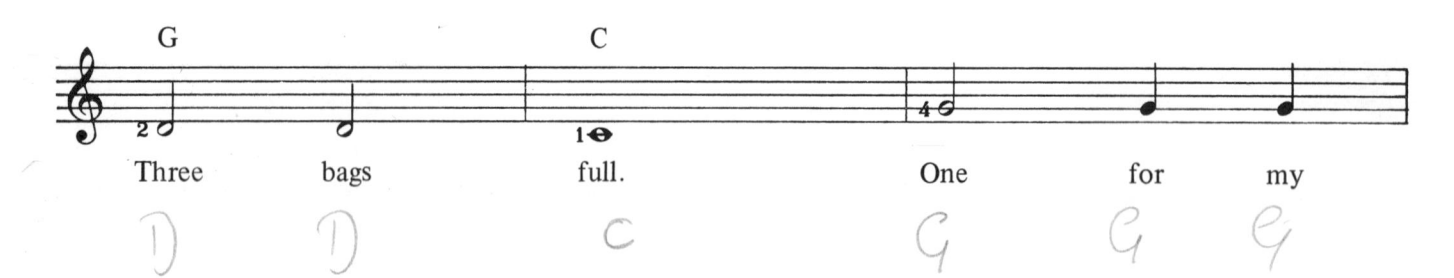

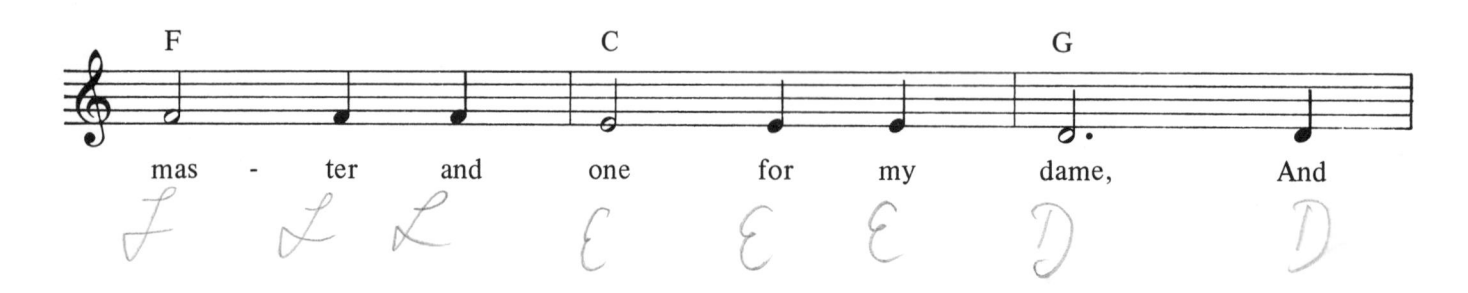

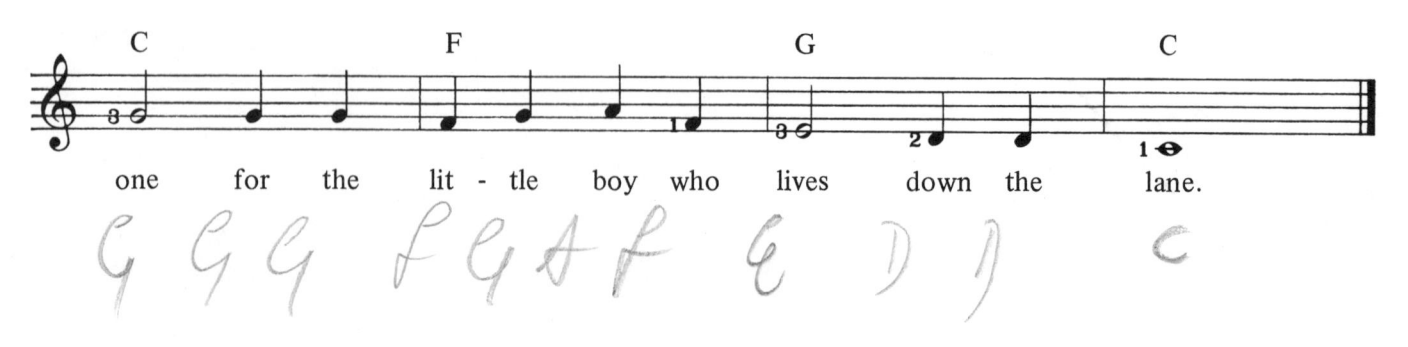

Baa baa black sheep, Have you an-y wool? Yes, sir, yes, sir, Three bags full. One for my mas-ter and one for my dame, And one for the lit-tle boy who lives down the lane.

Boys And Girls Come Out To Play

Flute/Clarinet or Organ
Waltz (Fairly Fast)

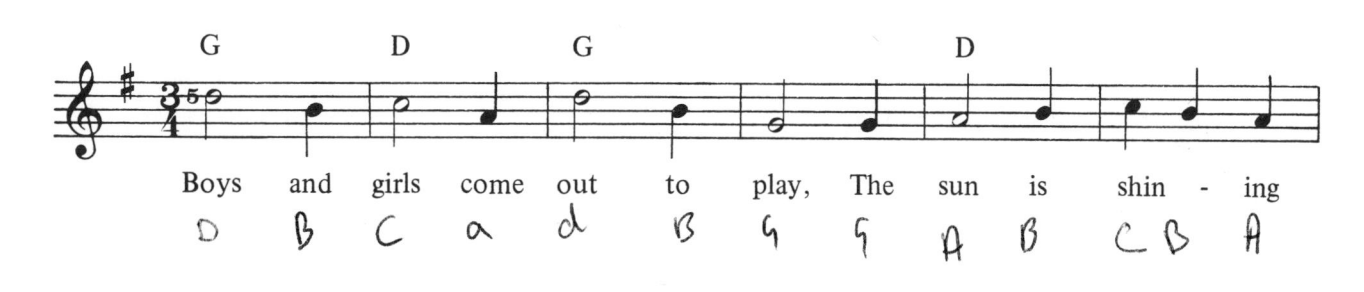

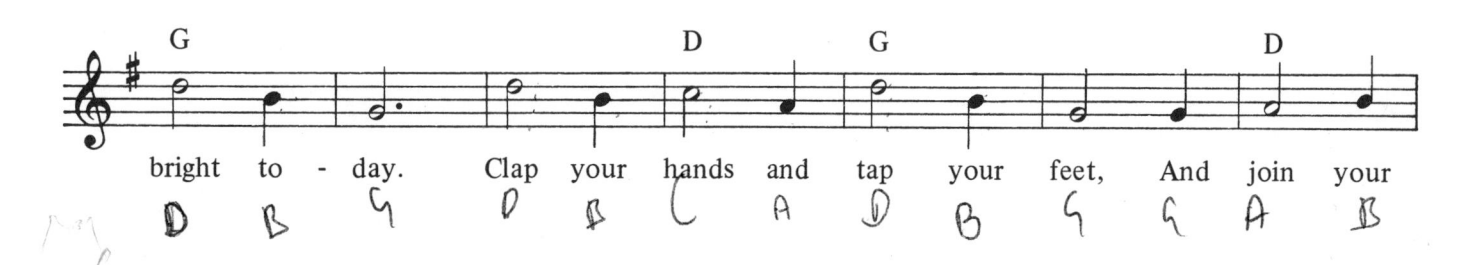

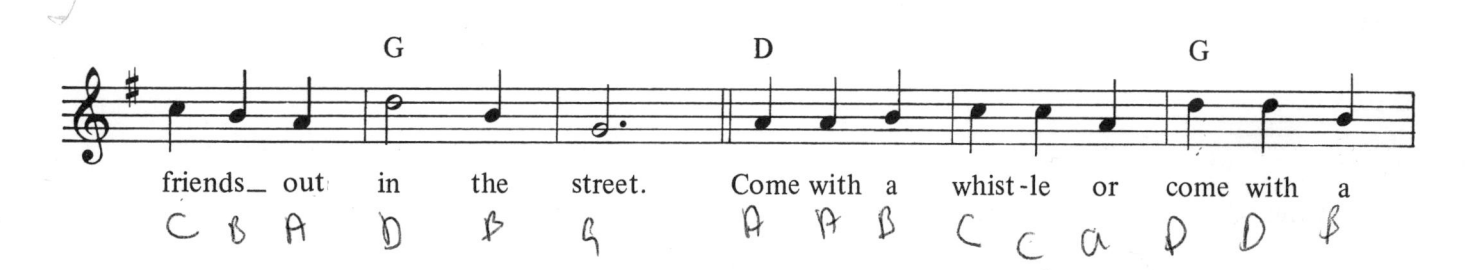

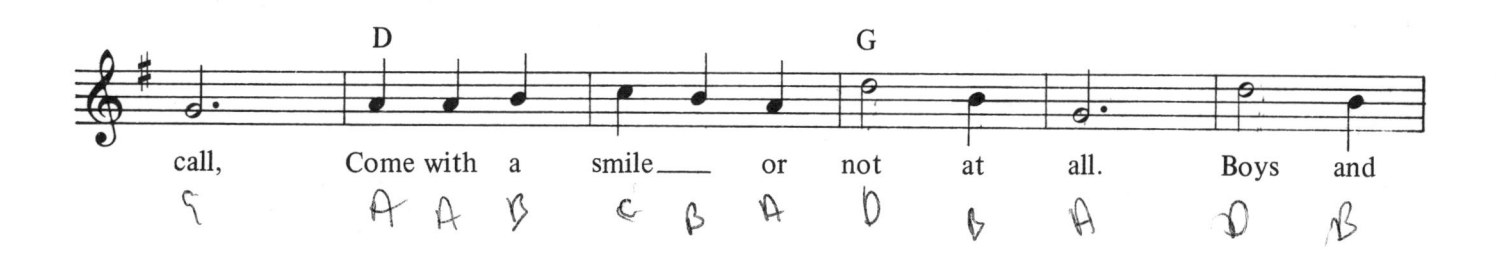

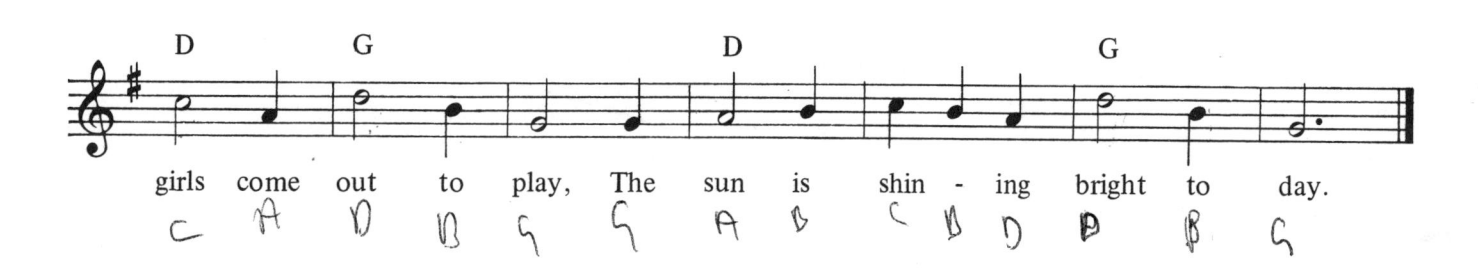

Boys and girls come out to play, The sun is shin - ing
bright to - day. Clap your hands and tap your feet, And join your
friends out in the street. Come with a whist-le or come with a
call, Come with a smile or not at all. Boys and
girls come out to play, The sun is shin - ing bright to day.

© 1986 International Music Publications, Woodford Green, Essex IG8 8HN

Goosey, Goosey Gander

Vibes (Vibraphone) or Piano
Ballad/Pops or Rock (Medium - Slow)

Goo - sey, goo - sey gan - der, Where do you wan - der?
Up - stairs and down - stairs, And in my la - dy's cham - ber.
There I met an old man who would - n't say his prayers; So I
took him by the left leg and threw him down the stairs.

Goosey, goosey gander,
Where do you wander?
Upstairs and downstairs,
And in my lady's chamber.

There I met an old man
Who wouldn't say his prayers;
So I took him by the left leg,
And threw him down the stairs.

© 1986 International Music Publications, Woodford Green, Essex IG8 8HN

The Grand Old Duke Of York

Trumpet/Trombone/Brass
March or Ballad/Pops (Medium)

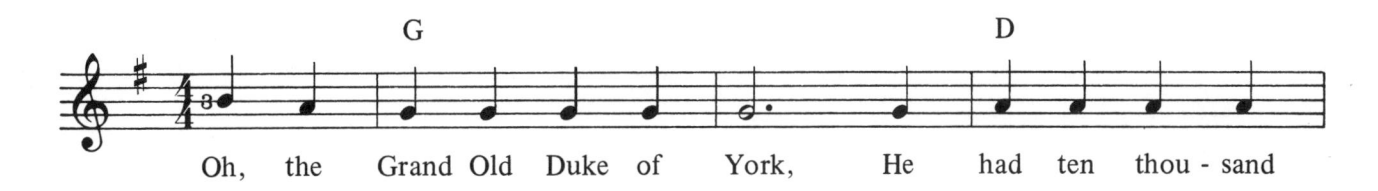

Oh, the Grand Old Duke of York, He had ten thou-sand men, He marched them up to the top of the hill, And he marched them down a-gain. And when they were up they were up; And when they were down they were down, And when they were on-ly half way up, They were nei-ther up nor down!

Here We Go Round The Mulberry Bush

Trumpet/Trombone/Brass or Organ
Waltz (Medium - Fast)

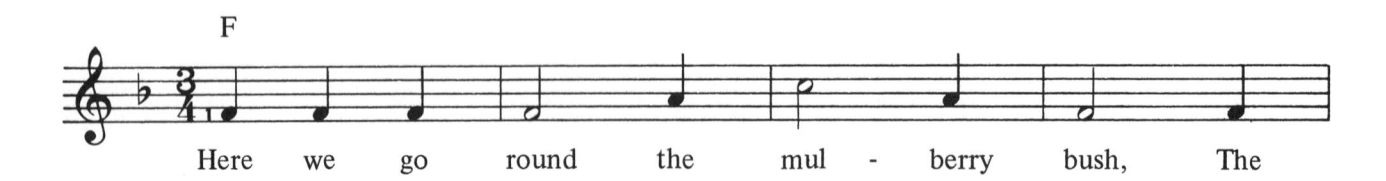

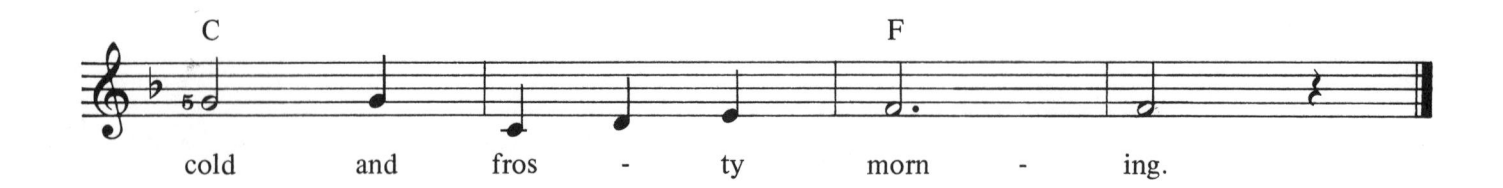

Here we go round the mul - berry bush, The mul - berry bush, The mul - berry bush.

Here we go round the mul - berry bush, On a cold and fros - ty morn - ing.

2. This is the way we wash our hands,
   Wash our hands, Wash our hands.
   This is the way we wash our hands,
   On a cold and frosty morning.

3. This is the way we clean our teeth...

4. This is the way we brush our hair...

5. Here we go round the mulberry bush...

8   © 1986 International Music Publications, Woodford Green, Essex IG8 8HN

Hey Diddle Diddle

Violin/Strings
Waltz (Medium) (Arpeggio)

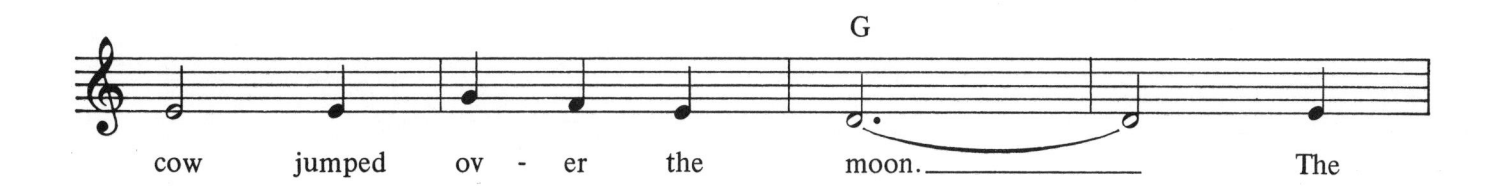

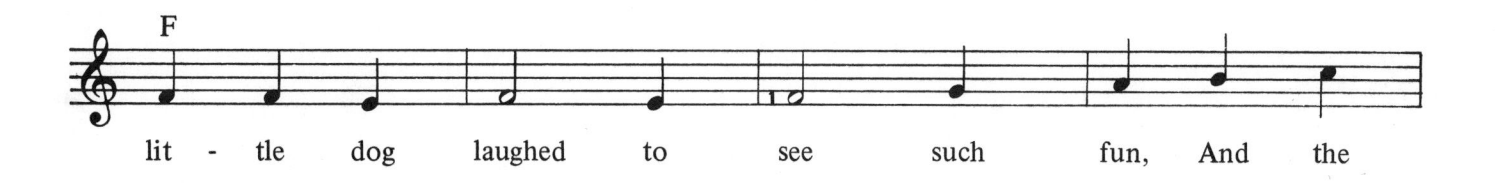

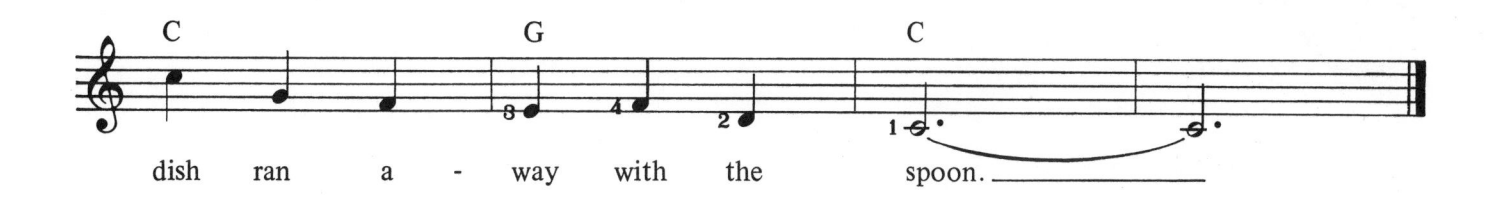

Hey did-dle did-dle, The cat and the fid-dle, The cow jumped ov-er the moon. The lit-tle dog laughed to see such fun, And the dish ran a-way with the spoon.

Hey diddle diddle,
The cat and the fiddle,
The cow jumped over the moon.
The little dog laughed
To see such fun,
And the dish ran away with the spoon.

Hickory Dickory Dock

Guitar or Trumpet/Brass
Waltz (Medium)

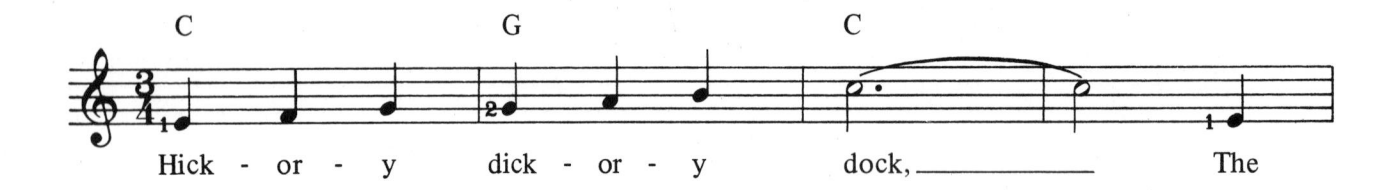

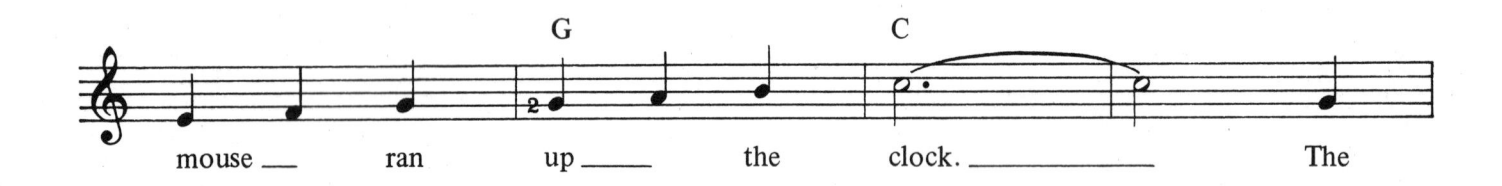

Hick - or - y dick - or - y dock, ____ The

mouse ___ ran up ___ the clock. ____ The

clock struck 'one', the mouse ran down,

Hick - or - y dick - or - y dock. ____

Hickory, dickory, dock,
The mouse ran up the clock.
The clock struck 'one',
The mouse ran down,
Hickory, dickory, dock.

Humpty Dumpty

Clarinet/Flute or Organ
Waltz (Medium)

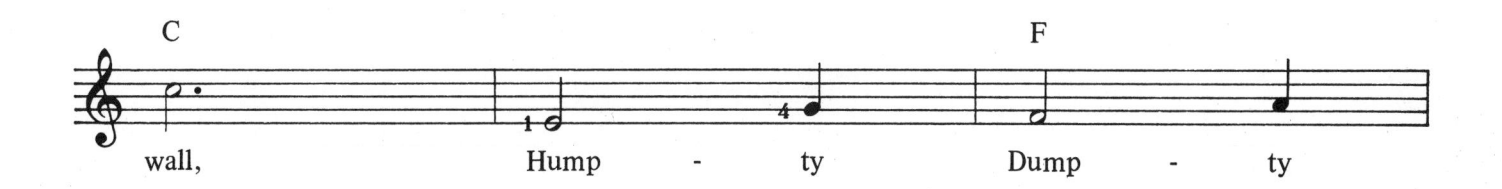

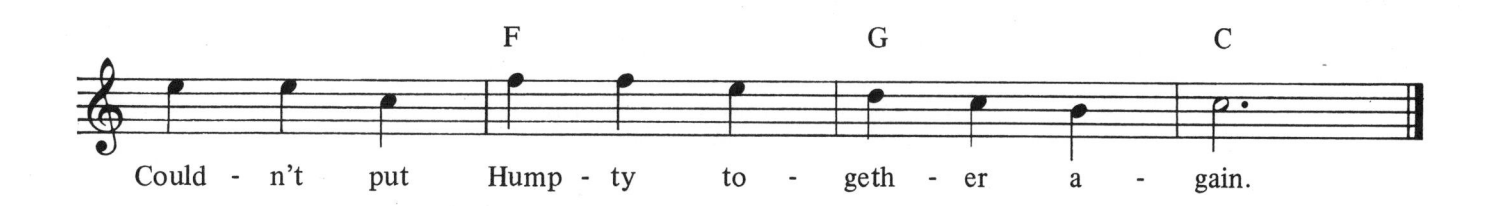

Jack And Jill

Flute/Clarinet or Organ
Waltz (Medium - Fast) (Arpeggio)

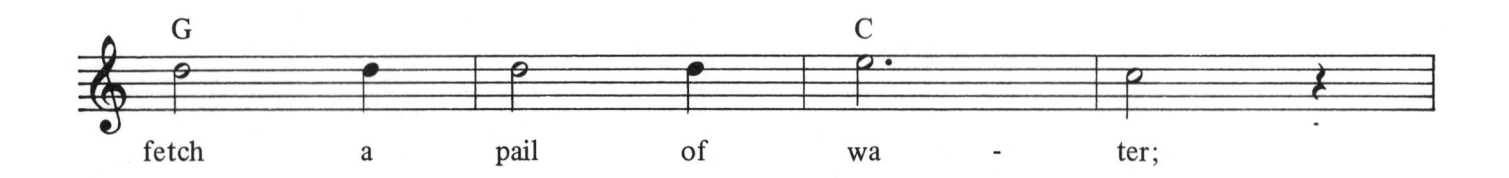

Jack and Jill went up the hill, To fetch a pail of wa - ter; Jack fell down and broke his crown, And Jill came tum - bling af - ter.

2. Up Jack got and home did trot,
   As fast as he could caper;
   He went to bed, and wrapped his head
   In vinegar and brown paper.

Little Bo Peep

Organ
Waltz (Medium) (Arpeggio)

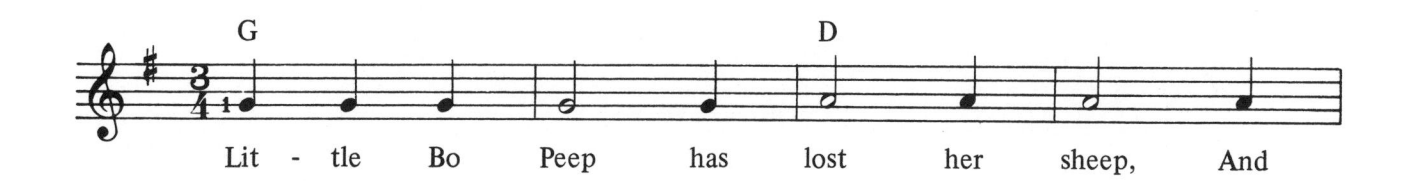

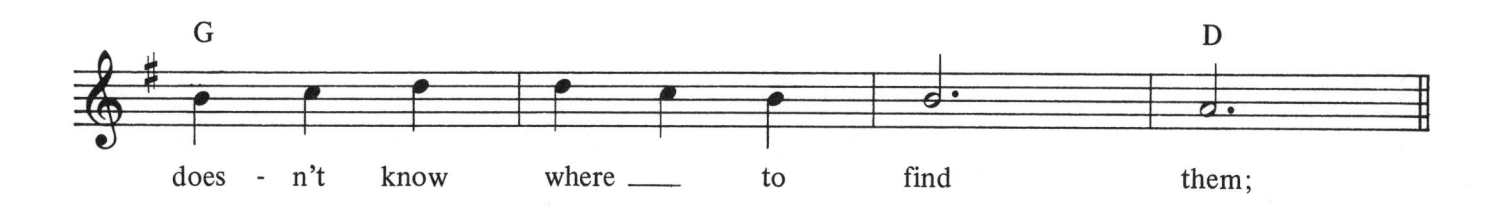

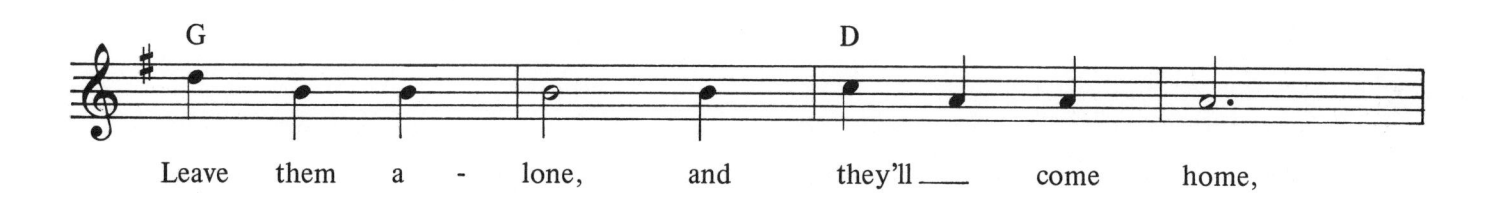

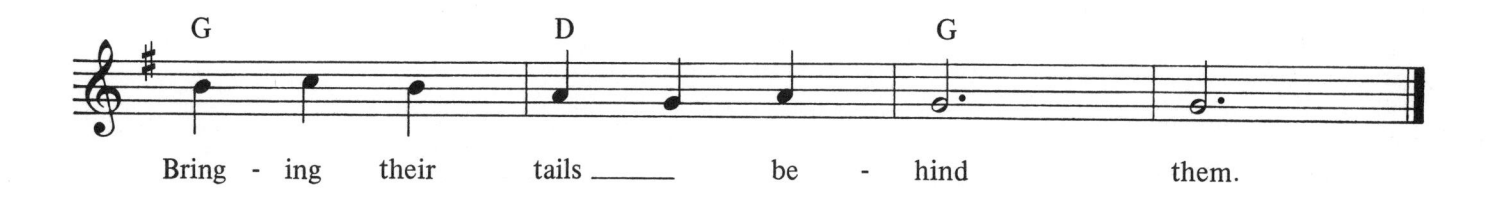

Lit - tle Bo Peep has lost her sheep, And does - n't know where to find them; Leave them a - lone, and they'll come home, Bring - ing their tails be - hind them.

2. Little Bo Peep fell fast asleep,
   And dreamt she heard them bleating;
   But when she awoke, she found it a joke,
   For they were still all a-fleeting.

3. Then up she took her little crook,
   Determined that she would find them;
   She found them indeed, but it made her heart bleed,
   For they'd left their tails behind them.

Little Jack Horner
and 'Little Miss Muffet'

Flute/Clarinet or Organ
Waltz (Medium) (Arpeggio)

The same tune is used for 'Little Miss Muffet':

Little Miss Muffet,
Sat on a tuffet,
Eating her curds and whey;
Along came a spider,
Who sat down beside her,
And frightened Miss Muffet away.

London Bridge Is Falling Down

Flute/Clarinet or Organ
March or Ballad/Pops (Fairly fast)

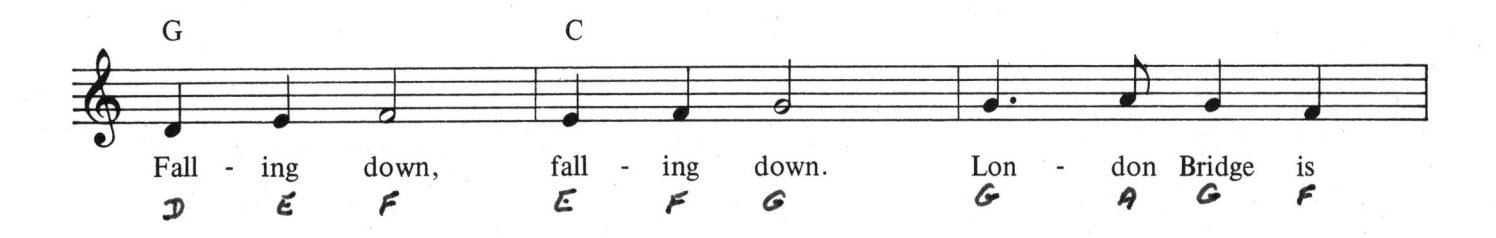

Lon - don Bridge is fall - ing down,
G A G F E F G

Fall - ing down, fall - ing down. Lon - don Bridge is
D E F E F G G A G F

fall - ing down, My fair la - dy.
E F G D G E C

2. Shall we build it up again,
   Up again, up again?
   Shall we build it up again,
   My fair lady?

3. Build it up with iron and steel...

4. Iron and steel will bend and break...

5. Then build it up with bricks and stone...

6. That will last a long long time...

Mary, Mary, Quite Contrary

Vibes (Vibraphone) or Trumpet/Brass
Ballad/Pops or Rock (Medium - Slow)

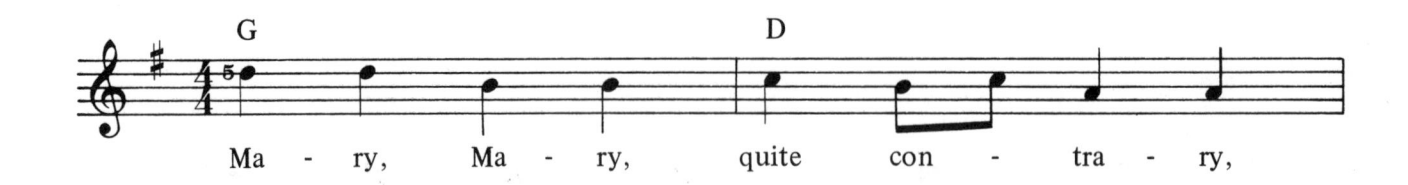

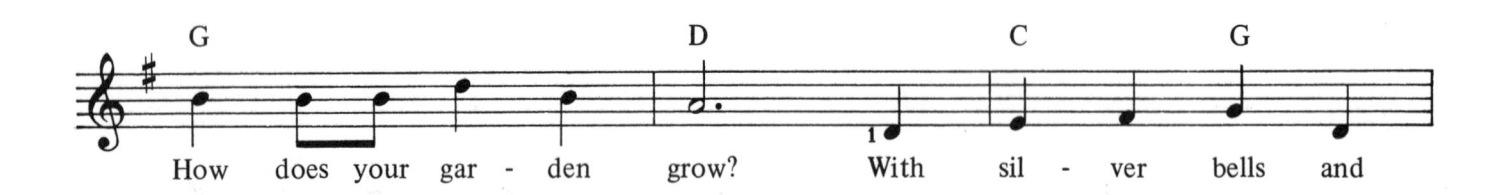

Ma - ry, Ma - ry, quite con - tra - ry,
How does your gar - den grow? With sil - ver bells and
cock - le shells, And pret - ty maids all in a row, And
pret - ty maids all in a row.

Mary, Mary, quite contrary,
How does your garden grow?
With silver bells and cockle shells,
And pretty maids all in a row,
And pretty maids all in a row.

© 1986 International Music Publications, Woodford Green, Essex IG8 8HN

Michael Finnigin

Trumpet/Guitar or Jazz Organ/Organ 2
Swing or Ballad/Pops/Rock (Medium)

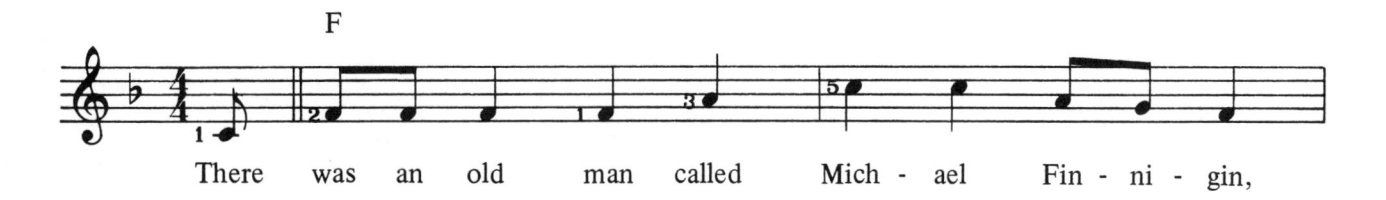

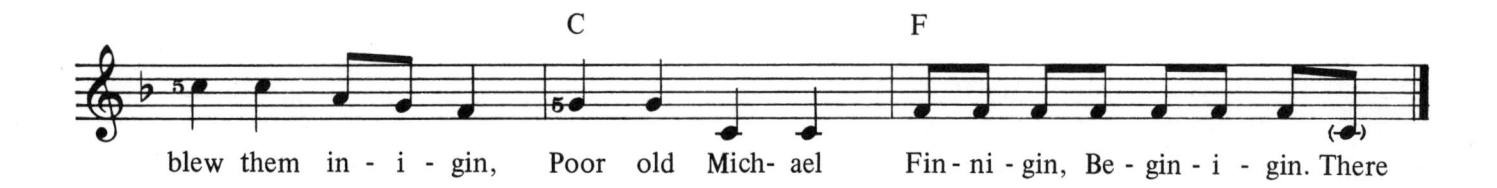

There was an old man called Mich - ael Fin - ni - gin,
He grew whis - kers on his chin - i - gin, The wind came up and
blew them in - i - gin, Poor old Mich- ael Fin - ni - gin, Be - gin - i - gin. There

2. There was an old man called Michael Finnigin,
   Climbed a tree and barked his shin-i-gin,
   Took off several yards of skin-i-gin,
   Poor old Michael Finnigin, Begin-i-gin.

3. There was an old man called Michael Finnigin,
   He went fishing with a pin-i-gin,
   Caught a fish, but dropped it in-i-gin,
   Poor old Michael Finnigin, Begin-i-gin.

4. There was an old man called Michael Finnigin,
   He grew fat and then grew thin-i-gin,
   Then he died and had to begin-i-gin,
   Poor old Michael Finnigin, Begin-i-gin!

Old MacDonald Had A Farm

Violin/Strings
Swing or Rock/Ballad/Pops (Medium)

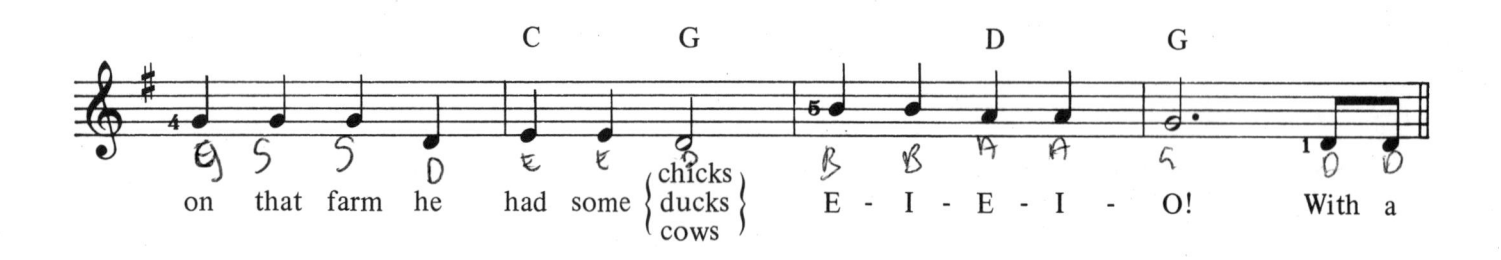

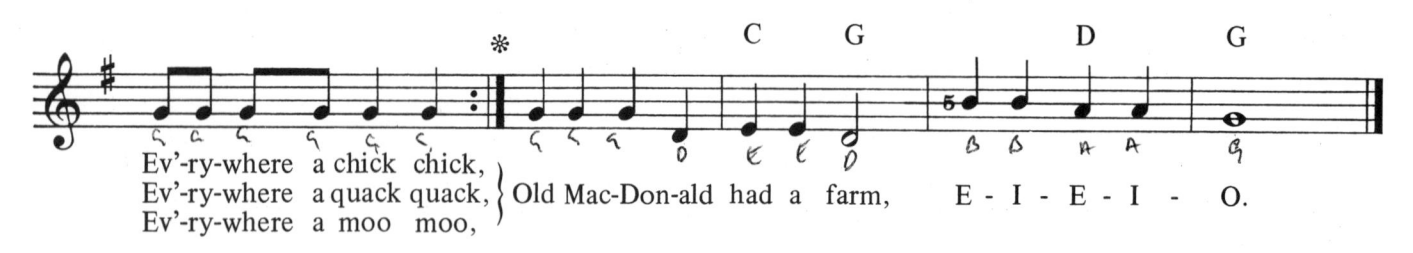

(Repeat previous verses. ✱ ——— ✱)

4. ...some sheep......with a baa baa...

5. ...some pigs......with an oink oink...

6. ...some turkeys...with a gobble gobble...

7. ...a car.........with a beep beep...

One Man Went To Mow

Trumpet/Brass
Rock/Ballad/Pops or Swing (Medium) (Handclap)

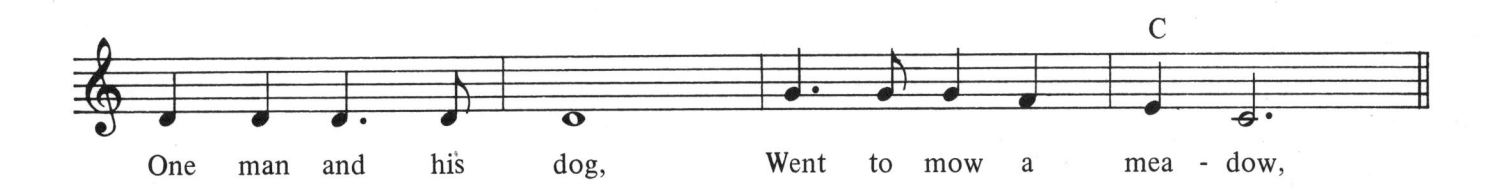

*Repeat the words from previous verses:

3. Three men, *two men, one man and his dog...*

4. Four men, *three men, two men, one man and his dog...*

© 1986 International Music Publications, Woodford Green, Essex IG8 8HN

Oranges And Lemons

Vibes (Vibraphone)/Piano or Guitar
Waltz (Medium) (Arpeggio)

Or - an - ges and lem - ons, say the bells of St. Cle - ment's; You owe me five far - things, say the bells of St. Mar - tin's When will you pay me? say the bells of Old Bai - ley. When I grow rich, say the bells of Shore - ditch. When will that be? — say the bells of Step - ney. — I'm sure I don't know, says the great bell of Bow.

Pat-A-Cake

Violin/Strings
Waltz (Medium) (Arpeggio)

Pat - a - cake, pat - a - cake, ba - ker's man,
Bake me a cake as fast as you can.
Pat it and prick it, and mark it with 'B', And
put it in the ov - en for ba - by and me. Yes,
put it in the ov - en for ba - by and me.

© 1986 International Music Publications, Woodford Green, Essex IG8 8HN

Polly Put The Kettle On

Vibes (Vibraphone)/Guitar or Trumpet
Rock/Ballad/Pops or March (Medium)

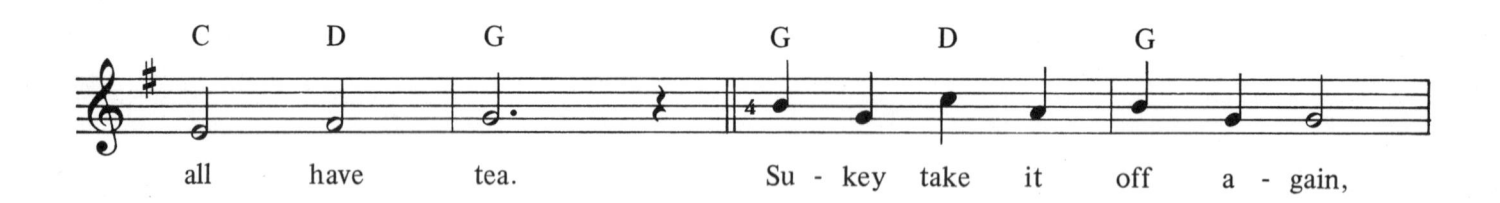

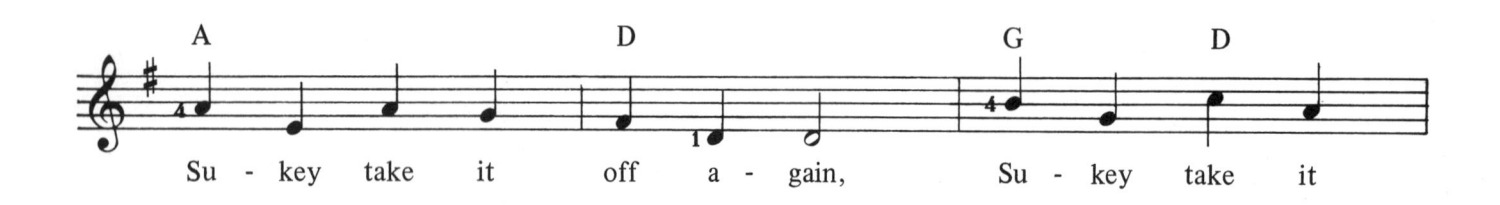

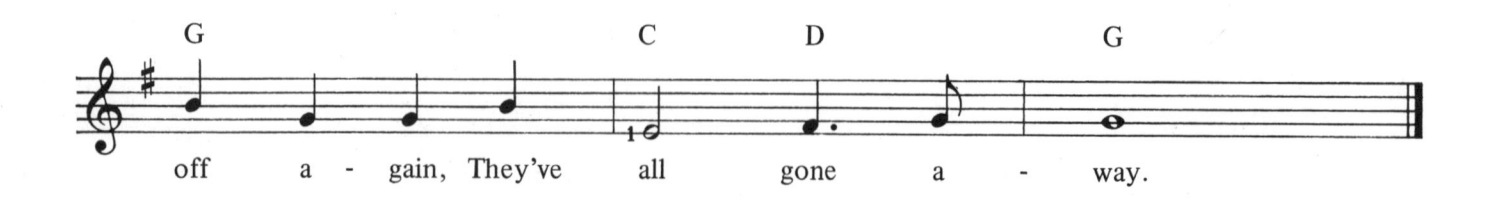

Pol - ly put the ket - tle on, Pol - ly put the ket - tle on, Pol - ly put the ket - tle on, We'll all have tea. Su - key take it off a - gain, Su - key take it off a - gain, Su - key take it off a - gain, They've all gone a - way.

Pop! Goes The Weasel

Trumpet/Brass or Guitar
Waltz (Medium) - or play with rhythm switched off

© 1986 International Music Publications, Woodford Green, Essex IG8 8HN

Rock-A-Bye Baby

Organ
Waltz (Medium - Slow) (Arpeggio)

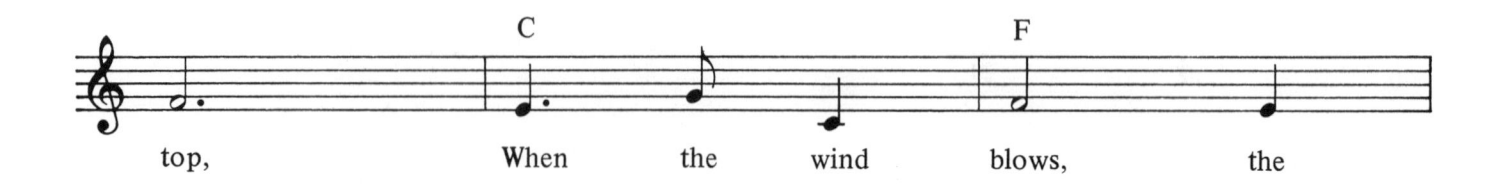

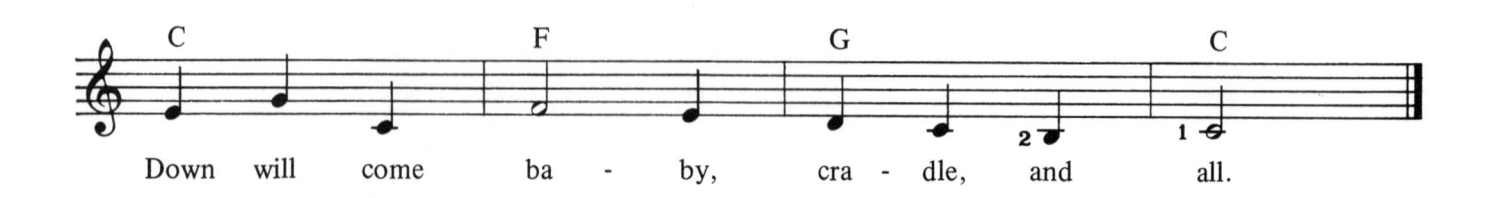

Rock - a - bye, ba - by, on the tree top, When the wind blows, the cra - dle will rock. When the bough breaks, the cra - dle will fall, Down will come ba - by, cra - dle, and all.

She'll Be Coming Round The Mountain

Violin/Strings
Swing (Medium) (Handclap)

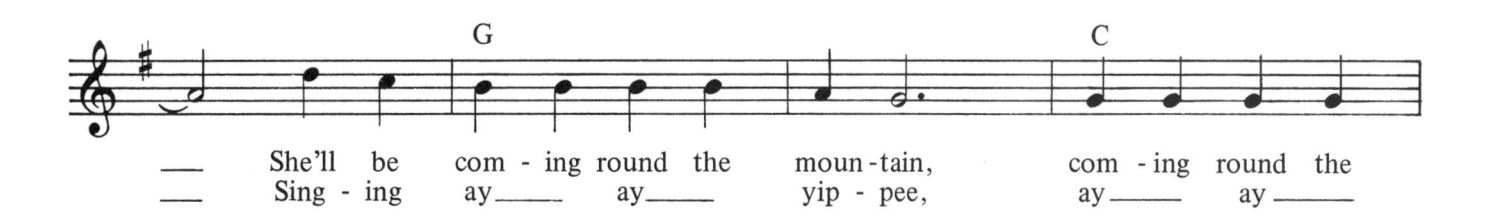

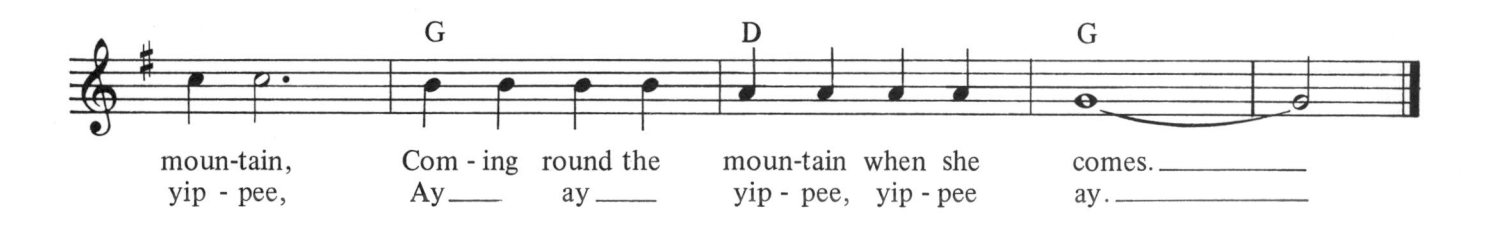

Chorus:

She'll be com-ing round the moun-tain when she comes,
Sing-ing ay ay yip-pee, yip-pee, ay,

She'll be com-ing round the moun-tain when she comes;
Sing-ing ay ay yip-pee, yip-pee, ay,

She'll be com-ing round the moun-tain, com-ing round the
Sing-ing ay ay yip-pee, ay ay

moun-tain, Com-ing round the moun-tain when she comes.
yip-pee, Ay ay yip-pee, yip-pee ay.

2. She'll be driving six white horses when she comes...

3. She'll be wearing pink pyjamas when she comes...

4. We will all be together when she comes...

© 1986 International Music Publications, Woodford Green, Essex IG8 8HN

25

Sing A Song Of Sixpence

Flute/Organ
Ballad/Pops or Rock (Medium)

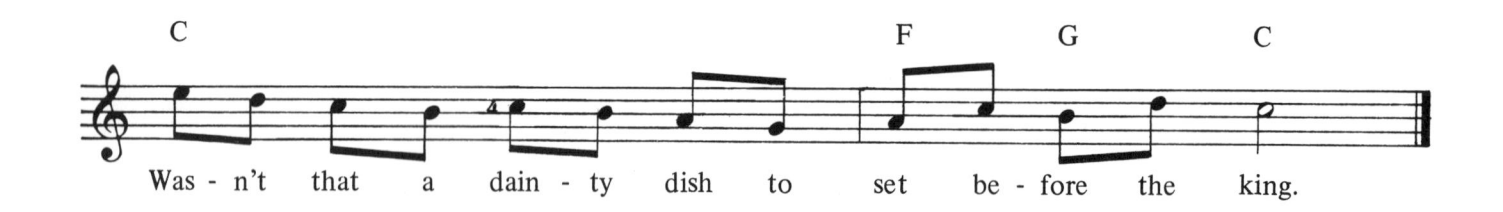

Sing a song of six - pence a pock - et full of rye,

Four and twen - ty black - birds baked in a pie;

When the pie was o - pened the birds be - gan to sing,

Was - n't that a dain - ty dish to set be - fore the king.

    2. The king was in the counting house,
       Counting out his money;
       The queen was in the parlour,
       Eating bread and honey.

       The maid was in the garden,
       Hanging out the clothes,
       When down came a blackbird,
       And pecked off her nose.

© 1986 International Music Publications, Woodford Green, Essex IG8 8HN

Ten Green Bottles

Clarinet/Flute or Organ
Rock/Ballad/Pops or March (Medium) - or play with rhythm switched off

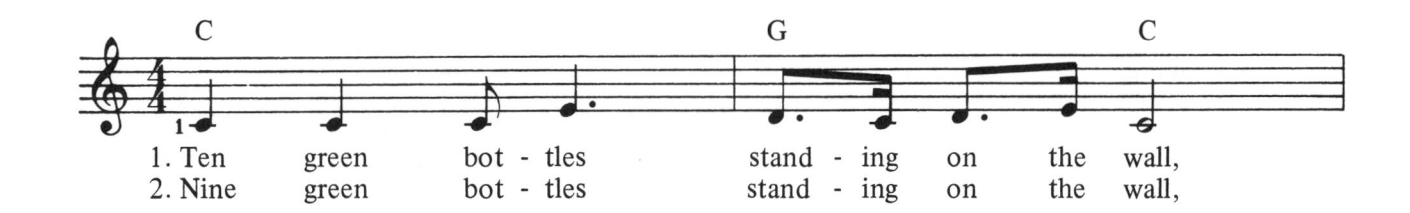

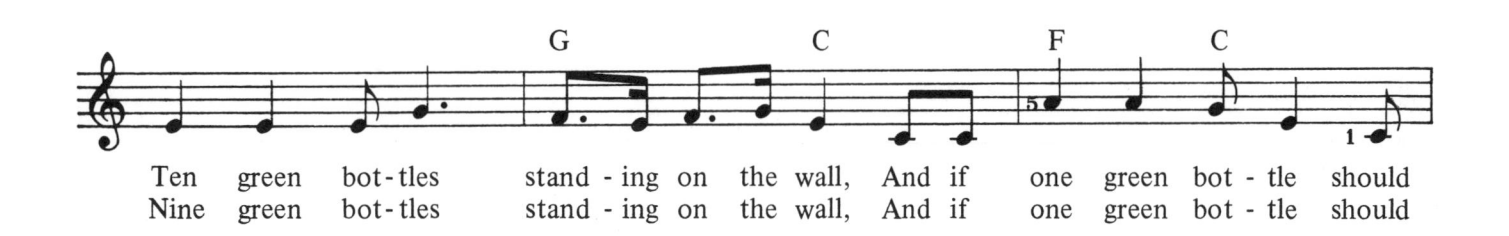

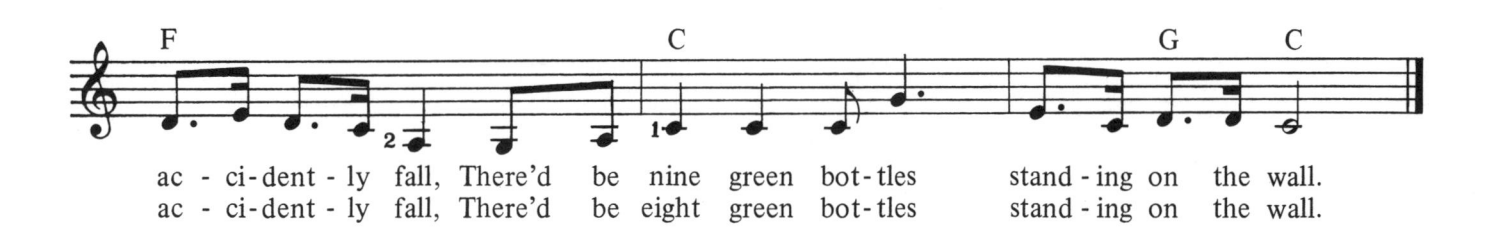

1. Ten green bot-tles stand-ing on the wall,
2. Nine green bot-tles stand-ing on the wall,

Ten green bot-tles stand-ing on the wall, And if one green bot-tle should
Nine green bot-tles stand-ing on the wall, And if one green bot-tle should

ac-ci-dent-ly fall, There'd be nine green bot-tles stand-ing on the wall.
ac-ci-dent-ly fall, There'd be eight green bot-tles stand-ing on the wall.

Eight green bottles . . . . seven green bottles standing, on the wall.

Seven green bottles . . . six green bottles standing on the wall.

Six green bottles . . . . . . five green bottles standing on the wall.

Five green bottles. . . . . . four green bottles standing on the wall.

Four green bottles . . . . three green bottles standing on the wall.

Three green bottles . . . two green bottles standing on the wall.

Two green bottles . . . . one green bottle standing on the wall.

One green bottle . . . . . no green bottles standing on the wall.

© 1986 International Music Publications, Woodford Green, Essex IG8 8HN

There's A Hole In My Bucket

Violin/Strings
Waltz (Medium)

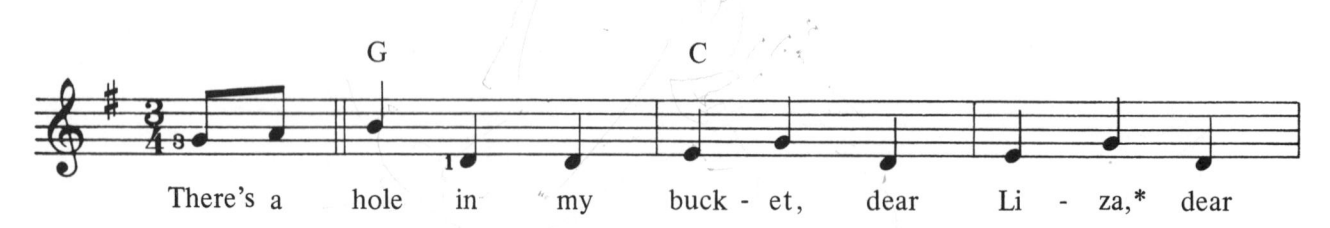

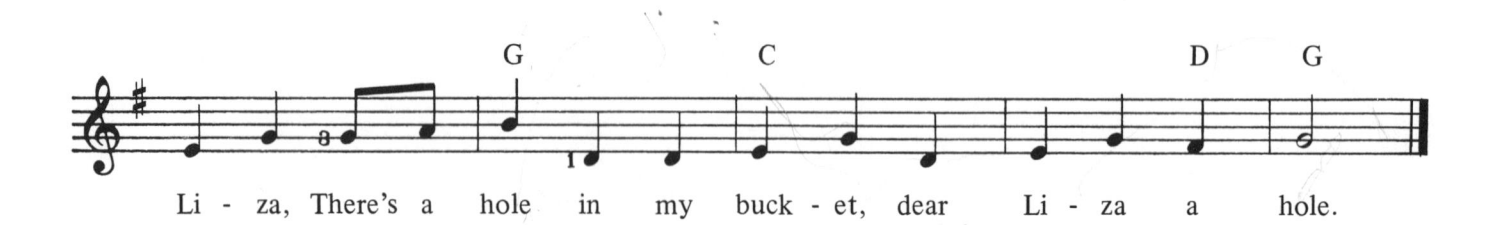

There's a hole in my buck-et, dear Li - za,* dear Li - za, There's a hole in my buck-et, dear Li - za a hole.

Then mend it, dear Henry,* dear Henry, dear Henry,
Then mend it dear Henry, dear Henry, mend it!
With what shall I mend it, dear Liza? .... with what?
With a straw, dear Henry .... with a straw.
But the straw is too long, dear Liza ..... too long.
Then cut it, dear Henry, ... cut it!
With what shall I cut it, dear Liza? ...... with what?
With a knife, dear Henry .... with a knife!
But the knife is too blunt, dear Liza .... too blunt.
Then sharpen it, dear Henry .... sharpen it!
With what shall I sharpen it, dear Liza? .. with what?
With a stone, dear Henry .... with a stone.
But the stone is too dry, dear Liza ...... too dry.
Then wet it, dear Henry .... wet it!
With what shall I wet it, dear Liza? ..... with what?
With water, dear Henry .... with water!
In what shall I get it, dear Liza? .... in what?
In a bucket, dear Henry .... in a bucket!
But there's a hole in my bucket, dear Liza.. a hole!

*You can change the names to suit the singers, or use the names of your family or friends.

This Old Man

Flute/Clarinet or Organ
Ballad/Pops or Rock (Medium) (Handclap)

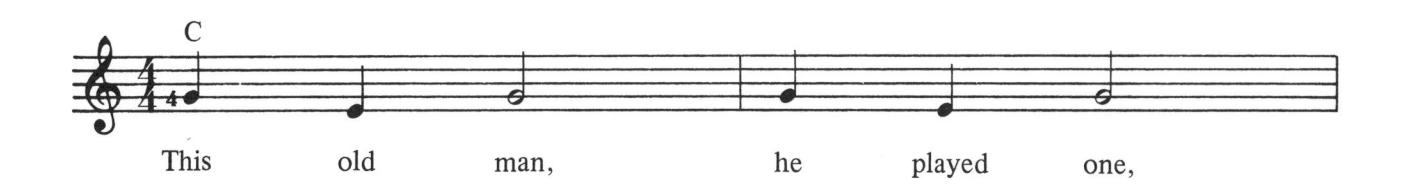

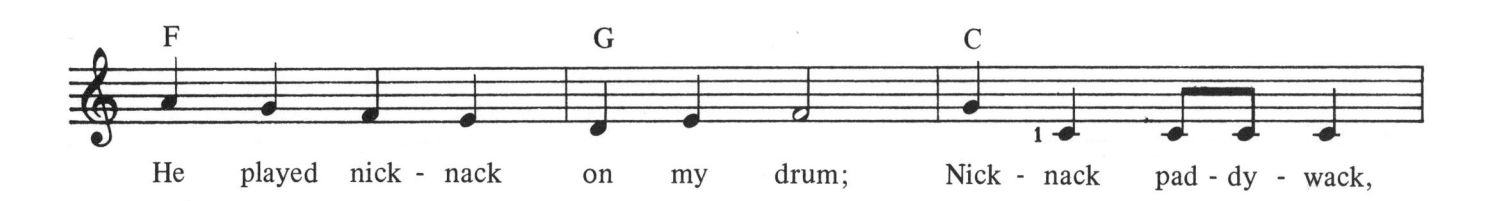

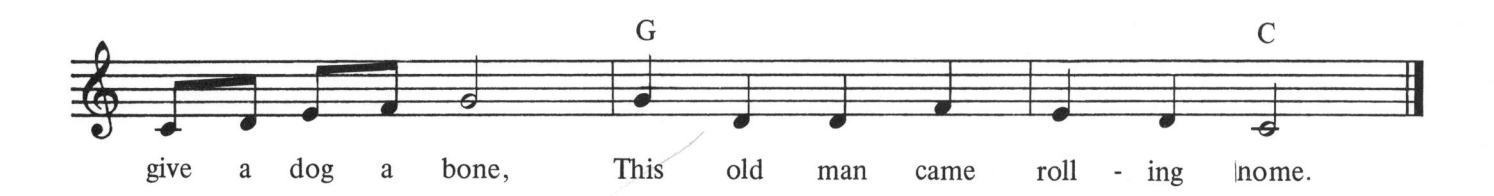

This old man, he played one,
He played nick-nack on my drum;
Nick-nack pad-dy-wack, give a dog a bone,
This old man came roll-ing home.

2. This old man, he played two,
   He played nick-nack on my shoe;
   Nick-nack paddy-wack, give a dog a bone,
   This old man came rolling home.

3. This old man, he played three,
   He played nick-nack on a tree,
   Nick-nack paddy-wack, give a dog a bone,
   This old man came rolling home.

4. This old man, he played four,
   He played nick-nack on the door,
   Nick-nack paddy-wack, give a dog a bone,
   This old man came rolling home.

© 1986 International Music Publications, Woodford Green, Essex IG8 8HN

Three Blind Mice

Flute/Clarinet or Organ
Waltz (Medium - Fast) - or play with rhythm switched off

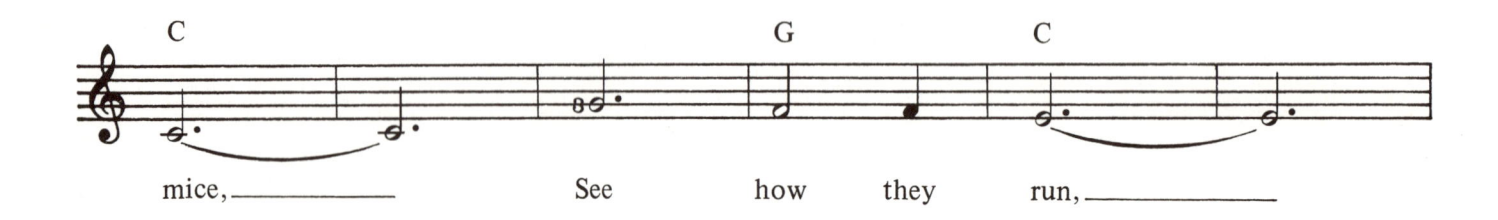

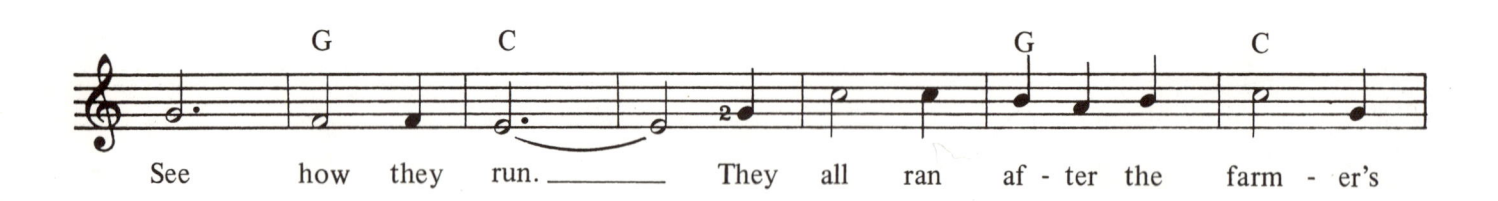

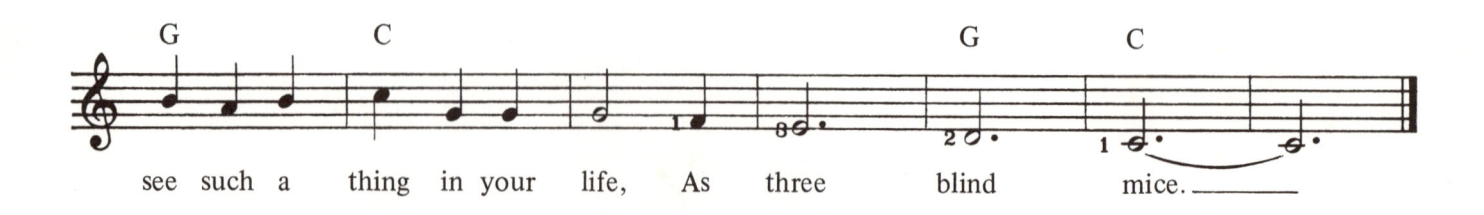

Three blind mice, ____ Three blind mice, ____ See how they run, ____ See how they run. ____ They all ran after the farmer's wife, Who cut off their tails with a carving knife, Did you ever see such a thing in your life, As three blind mice. ____

30   © 1986 International Music Publications, Woodford Green, Essex IG8 8HN

Twinkle, Twinkle, Little Star

Vibes (Vibraphone) or Piano
Ballad/Pops or Rock (Medium - Slow)

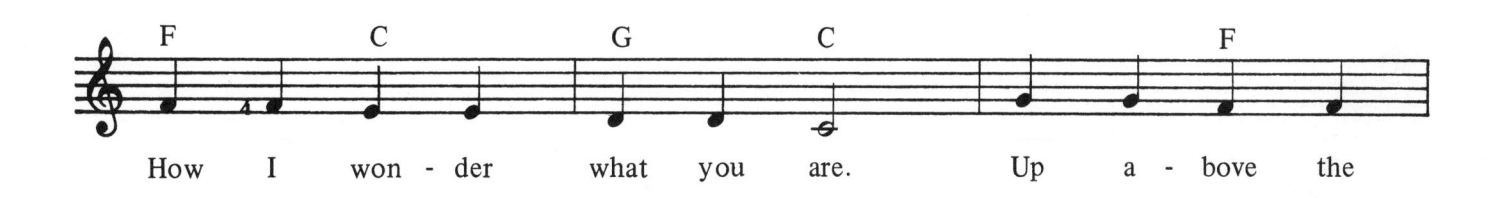

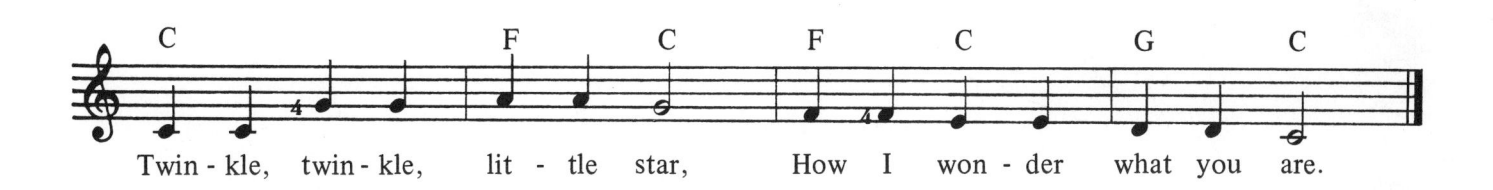

Twinkle, twinkle little star,
How I wonder what you are.
Up above the world so high,
Like a diamond in the sky.
Twinkle, twinkle little star,
How I wonder what you are.

© 1986 International Music Publications, Woodford Green, Essex IG8 8HN

Ask your music dealer for these easy-to-follow books by Roger Evans:

PLAYING KEYBOARDS — With Roger Evans & Vince Hill

All you need to know to play easy keyboard music.

With this one easy book you can start playing popular tunes on your keyboard in minutes — even if you know nothing about music before you begin.

PLAYING KEYBOARDS features hit songs: 'Flashdance . . . What A Feeling', 'Hello', 'Sloop John B', 'Send In The Clowns', 'Scarborough Fair', plus many other popular tunes to play. All specially arranged by Roger Evans.
Order Ref: 09948   ISBN 0 86359 264 3

PLAYING KEYBOARDS CASSETTE — Recorded by Roger Evans.

This entertaining and informative cattette takes you step by step through PLAYING KEYBOARDS, and makes learning even easier. You can hear each tune on the cassette and you can play along with the music whenever you wish.
Order Ref: 09967

PLAYING KEYBOARDS — SONGS & MUSIC BOOK 1

An exciting collection of hit songs made famous by such great performers as George Michael, Elton John, David Gates, Sting, John Lennon and Lionel Richie.
Plus popular keyboard music like 'Moonlight' and Scott Joplin's 'The Entertainer'. All specially arranged by Roger Evans.
Order Ref: 16043   ISBN 0 86359 292 9

PLAYING KEYBOARDS — SONGS & MUSIC BOOK 2

Song made famous by Stevie Wonder, Elton John, Lionel Richie, U.B. 40, Bee Gees, and other outstanding artists.
Plus the Theme from 'Cats', 'Chariots Of Fire' and many other popular tunes. All specially arranged by Roger Evans.
Order Ref: 16287   ISBN 0 86359 359 3

PLAYING KEYBOARDS — CHRISTMAS SONGBOOK

'Mary's Boy Child', 'When A Child Is Born', 'Good King Wenceslas', 'Silent Night' — plus another twenty-one favourite Christmas songs and carols for you to enjoy with your family and friends.
Order Ref: 16329   ISBN 0 86359 362 3

Full words are given for each song, and these books are complete with 'one finger chords' and helpful playing hints.

ABOUT THE AUTHOR:

Roger Evans is well known for his best selling musical books which are published in Britain, USA, Japan, Spain, Australia and other countries, and sold throughout the world.

Other popular Roger Evans books include *How To Read Music, How To Play Piano, How To Play Guitar, Beginners Guitar Book* and *Starting To Play Guitar* cassette and book.